WHO, WHAT, WHY

WHAT WA

The Underground Railroad?

DANIKA COOLEY

CF4·K

10 9 8 7 6 5 4 3 2 1
Copyright © Danika Cooley 2023
Paperback ISBN: 978-1-5271-1010-6
ebook ISBN: 978-1-5271-1078-6

Published by
Christian Focus Publications,
Geanies House, Fearn, Tain, Ross-shire,
IV20 1TW, Scotland, U.K.
www.christianfocus.com
email: info@christianfocus.com

Printed and bound by Bell and Bain, Glasgow

Cover design by Catriona Mackenzie
Illustrations by Martyn Smith

TABLE OF CONTENTS

Dedication

*To courageous kids.
May you seek to obey God rather
than men.*

THE AUTHOR

Danika Cooley and her husband, Ed, are committed to leading their children to life for the glory of God. Danika has a passion for equipping parents to teach the Bible and Christian history to their kids. She is the author of *Help Your Kids Learn and Love the Bible, When Lightning Struck!: The Story of Martin Luther, Wonderfully Made: God's Story of Life from Conception to Birth*, and the *Who, What, Why?* Series about the history of our faith. Danika's three year Bible survey curriculum, Bible Road Trip™, is used by families around the world. Weekly, she encourages tens of thousands of parents to intentionally raise biblically literate children. Danika is a homeschool mother of four with a bachelor of arts degree from the University of Washington. Find her at ThinkingKidsBlog.org.

MODERN TRAINS
AND ANCIENT SLAVERY

Early in the life of the United States of America, the country was slowly expanding from the Atlantic Ocean toward the Pacific. America was mostly wilderness without street signs, cars, or even streets— just dirt roads if you were lucky. Traveling over land was difficult, so intelligent men tried intelligent things

and in 1831 the Mohawk & Hudson Railroad built one hundred miles of train tracks in New York State.

The first passengers on the Mohawk & Hudson line were in for an adventure. The railway placed thirty passengers in three stagecoaches mounted on train trucks. There was a wood-burning steam engine in front. Have you ever seen sparks fly from a campfire? Well, imagine riding a train while your clothes are on fire. Those passengers had an exciting story to tell after their first fiery train ride.

Americans read about the new trains roaring across the country in their newspapers. It was during this time—when everything seemed possible and trains filled the imagination of every American—that Tice Davids swam across the Ohio River. He would have borrowed a boat to row across the wide river, but there just wasn't time.

Tice's owner reached the Kentucky banks of the Ohio River just in time to see Tice crawl out of the river and disappear into the Ohio town of Ripley. The man rowed himself across the river and interviewed townspeople. Surely someone had seen a dripping, poorly clothed, runaway slave? They had not. Angry, the man traveled home and told friends that Tice must have disappeared on an underground road.

Abolitionists—people who wanted to abolish, or end, slavery—loved the railroad word picture. Fugitive slaves were disappearing from the South just like trains disappeared into underground tunnels. The Underground Railroad became the name of a secret system through which runaway slaves escaped north to freedom.

From the early 1800s, abolitionists had been hiding fugitives in their homes during the day and sending them to another home at night. Now, abolitionists called safehouses stations. Helpers were station masters and conductors, and the paths fugitives took to freedom were lines.

Passengers on the Underground Railroad often later became station masters or conductors, so the system continued to grow. Historical records list the names of over three thousand people working on the Railroad. Certainly, many more helped quietly. From 1830 to 1860, perhaps one hundred and fifty thousand people fled from slavery. That's about five thousand people every year. That's enough people to start a good-sized town.

Perhaps you're wondering if disobeying the law and helping people escape was right or biblical. That's a good question. Most abolitionists were Bible-reading, God-fearing Christians. But, many southern plantation owners also claimed to be Christians. They pointed to Bible verses that tell us to obey our government leaders since God put them in place. Then, they did wicked, unbiblical things to the people they enslaved.

Christian abolitionists from the North spoke and wrote about Exodus 21:16, where God's law says: "Whoever steals a man and sells him, and anyone found in possession of him, shall be put to death." They reminded slave owners that African Americans are made in God's image. God commands us to love our neighbors. Also, the sin of slavery led to more sin. For example, slaves were kept from God's Word and the good news of Jesus. Slaves were often not allowed to marry. Children were sold away from parents. God's good gift of family was destroyed.

When we have questions about living according to God's Word, we should always search the Bible. Nearly three thousand years ago, probably between 875 and 853 BC—that means Before Christ—there was an evil king in Israel named Ahab. Ahab's wife, Jezebel, was murdering God's prophets. So, Ahab's household manager, Obadiah, hid one hundred prophets in a cave. Obadiah risked his life to save the prophets. He also disobeyed the king and his wife. What does God's Word say about Obadiah? In 1 Kings 18:3, it says, "Now Obadiah feared the Lord greatly."

There's more. About nine hundred years later, after Jesus died and rose from the dead to free sinners who follow him from their sins, Peter and the apostles were teaching about Jesus in Jerusalem. The high priest demanded they stop talking about Jesus. Do you know what they said to this leader? You can read it in Acts 5:29. In the ESV it reads, "We must obey God rather than men." The Bible has even more examples of people disobeying leaders when their laws oppose God's laws.

Enslaving people is an evil sin that leads to even more sin. Christians believed they were loving their neighbors by helping them escape slavery. They believed obeying the laws of the land would cause them to sin. Enslaved Christians believed the people enslaving them were sinning wickedly. Escaping was simply righting a terrible wrong. They cried out to God in songs and prayers as they looked toward freedom— for themselves and for others.

This is the story of those believers and of the American Underground Railroad. Christians' faithful efforts to serve God and to love their neighbors helped lead to ungodly laws being overturned and to freedom for more than four million Americans.

ENDING ENSLAVEMENT

In 1688, American Quakers—members of a religious people who follow some of the Bible's teachings—protested slavery. Soon, Christians of all denominations began helping slaves escape. In 1850 the Fugitive Slave Law allowed southern slave owners to recapture slaves in the North. Free blacks were kidnapped, and northern whites were required to help recapture fugitives. There were insurrections, riots, and battles. It was a mess.

When a Christian lady named Harriet Beecher Stowe published a novel, Uncle Tom's Cabin, many imagined what it might be like to be enslaved for the first time. A few years later, the Supreme Court ruled that a man, Dred Scott, was property and not a citizen of the United States. People were outraged.

Over six hundred thousand Americans died in the Civil War as the North and South fought over the rights of states to make their own rules—especially rules over slavery. In January 1865, the Constitution was amended to forbid slavery in the United States.

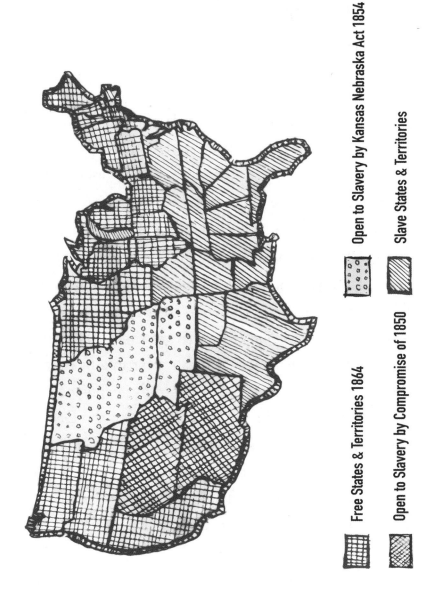

Free States & Territories 1864

Open to Slavery by Compromise of 1850

Open to Slavery by Kansas Nebraska Act 1854

Slave States & Territories

THIS WAY TO
FREEDOM

Have you ever taken a ride on a train? It can be a lot of fun. You board the train at a station, then enjoy the countryside as you race along the line. You disembark right where you intend to arrive.

Taking a ride on the Underground Railroad was a little different. Enslaved people fled their homes without a map, compass, or supplies. Most fugitives had never been far from home, so they didn't know where they were going or how to get there. They did know getting caught would mean a terrible beating, death, or, almost worse, being sold from the northern, midwestern, or southern border states into the Deep South. The states of the Deep South—South Carolina, Mississippi, Florida, Alabama, Georgia, Louisiana, and Texas—were a place of harsh slavery few escaped from. Every person a fugitive encountered could be an enemy, and probably was.

So why did they start their journey in the first place? Slavery was brutal. Often enslaved people fled after an especially terrible attack or beating. Jermain

Loguen left enslavement after his master badly injured his mouth with a wooden wedge. He later became a preacher and an Underground Railroad station master, helping others escape by hiding them and arranging their escape. Other slaves fled when they heard that they or their family members were about to be sold into the Deep South. Harriet Tubman, probably the most famous conductor on the Railroad, ran away when she believed she was about to be sold south of Maryland like her sisters had been. Conductors like Harriet led fugitives to safety.

Once on the road, fugitives faced danger—a lot of it. In border states, slave catchers patrolled roads and rivers, looking for people to capture for a reward. Groups of slave owners and hired men would use dogs to chase after fugitives. Then there were alligators, cougars, bears, poisonous snakes, and wolves. Anyone who made it past the animals had to worry about living through severe cold and hunger. Most slaves left without shoes or a jacket. They brought whatever food they could carry—if any at all.

Because of the dangers involved, most fugitives started their journeys on the weekend because they wouldn't be missed on Sunday. Sometimes they left while their owners were celebrating Christmas. That time of year was easier to be on the roads since many slaves were given passes to see family on neighboring farms during the holiday season.

For the most part, Underground Railroad lines—or routes—headed north to freedom at terminals—ending points—in northern states. Some refugees settled at terminals in Canada, where the British Government had declared all African Americans would be free Canadians.

It was safest to travel at night, so fugitives followed the North Star. On cloudy nights, they would hug trees, feeling for moss. North of the Equator, moss

tends to grow on the northern, shadier side of trees. South of the Equator, trees are shadier on the side facing south. In many places, the way was rugged and sparsely populated. Once fugitives came to towns or waterways, they had to decide who to ask for help. When a fugitive found an Underground Railroad operative, that's when they were truly riding the Underground Railroad.

Frederick Douglass, who became one of America's most famous abolitionists, escaped slavery by dressing as a sailor and boarding a train in Maryland. Next, he took a steamboat to Philadelphia and another train to New York. Wandering around New York City, Frederick was too afraid of meeting a slave catcher to ask for help. Finally, after days and nights spent on the streets, a sailor—a real one, not someone wearing a disguise like Frederick—found Frederick in a dangerous neighborhood and took him to station master David Ruggles' house. David, a free black man, helped Frederick marry his love, Anna, and start a new life in freedom.

Station masters would give fleeing slaves a place to spend the day, sleeping and resting. If fugitives were being pursued, station masters would feed their passengers and then send them onto the next station as quickly as possible. Underground Railroad lines were traveled in whatever manner could be arranged—on foot, in carriages or on trains, even hidden inside special wagon compartments beneath a load of hay. Often, fugitives escaped aboard ships. Sometimes the entire crew were enslaved African Americans.

When enslaved people did escape from the Deep South, which was rare, it was often aboard a ship. William Grimes, an enslaved man from Savannah, Georgia, was friends with the crew of the Brig Casket. He hid on the deck, buried in cotton bales. When the ship passed into free waters, his sailor friends gave three cheers to let him know he was a freed man.

Whenever they could, ship crew members would also escape to safety in the ports of free states. In fact, more than one out of every ten fugitives was a sailor. Maybe the Underground Railroad should have been called the Steamboat Lane.

Riding the lines of the Underground Railroad was dangerous and unpredictable. The lines, or routes to freedom, changed often with circumstances. Over time, the lines became clearer and easier for passengers to follow as they traced the North Star across rivers and through mountains to the first stop on their way.

Sometimes, conductors like Harriet Tubman risked journeying into the South to lead people to northern freedom. In whatever way fugitives reached their first stop, once they found a secret station, station masters and conductors helped point them to each new station on the way to a terminal, their last stop on the journey.

NOT EVERY TRAIN GOES NORTH

Fugitives from the Deep South sometimes fled to Mexico or joined Native American tribes. Others escaped to maroon colonies—secret communities where fugitives lived in swamps or forests. During the American Revolution, enslaved Americans even escaped with British troops.

George Liele preached Jesus to his fellow slaves and started the first black church in America in Savannah, Georgia. When George's former owner died during the Revolution, George—who had been freed to spend time preaching—was in danger of re-enslavement. So, George and his family sailed for Jamaica with the British, where he became the first modern missionary.

George asked English Baptist missionaries to come help him teach the thousands of new Jamaican Christians. A missionary named William Knibb sailed to Jamaica to help. After a slave revolt in Jamaica, called the Baptist War because slave owners blamed it on missionaries, William told people in England of the horrible abuses by the plantation owners. As a result, England freed all slaves.

PAYING FOR
TICKETS

Have you ever traveled with your family? Trips can be rather expensive. There is food to pay for and travel costs to cover. You may even need new shoes for your journey. Travelers need money.

Slaves, as a rule, don't have much money. That's because slave owners force enslaved people to work but don't pay them. It is stealing. Because people escaped with nothing, Underground Railroad workers supplied clothing, food, and even train tickets for their passengers. To do so, they needed funding.

The word *vigilance* means to stay on guard against danger. Beginning in the 1820s and 1830s, African Americans in northern cities like Boston, New York, and Philadelphia started vigilance committees to manage Underground Railroad activities. Vigilance committees watched for kidnappers, alerting communities whenever slave catchers were in town. Sometimes, they put posters in shop windows with the name of the slave catcher to look for.

African Americans, like William Still in Philadelphia and David Ruggles—who helped Frederick Douglass—in New York, managed the biggest stations in the biggest cities. They received incoming passengers and forwarded them on to the next station. Vigilance committees even hired lawyers to defend re-captured fugitives.

Women aren't mentioned often in the records of the Underground Railroad, but they worked just as hard as men to obey God rather than the laws of man. Women fed and hid fugitives, getting up in the middle of the night for each new arrival. A few women, like Harriet Tubman and schoolteacher Delia Webster, served as conductors—they traveled to the South to bring enslaved families to freedom.

Women also served on vigilance committees. They held antislavery fairs to raise money, selling handmade goods and fancy clothes from overseas. Abolitionist women also sewed dresses and suits for newly arrived fugitives to wear so they would be warm and comfortable, and so they would look just like every other northerner.

Even with all this fundraising work, more was needed. Good history detectives, like you, will notice there are names that pop up in history over and over again. Now, in the case of the abolition movement, there are three men you'll encounter who made a big difference. They also purchased a lot of tickets for passengers on the Underground Railroad.

Think of the most money you can imagine. Gerrit Smith probably had more. Gerrit had piles of inherited wealth just waiting for a purpose. He also had a lot of land. In fact, Gerrit was one of the richest men in America. Gerrit also had a deep love for Jesus and for all people made in God's image. Because Gerrit worked alongside his father's slaves when he was a boy, he had a special heart for people who were enslaved.

The Bible tells us that everything we have comes from God. We are to be good stewards—that means managers—of the resources we receive. Gerrit was a good steward. On the desk in his big mansion, he kept a pile of checks made

out for different amounts. When someone needed something—like a train ticket to Canada or to a little town for fugitives—Gerrit simply chose a check for the right amount and signed it. Gerrit also gave away land—lots and lots of land. To newly freed blacks in New York, he offered forty acres of farmland—each. Gerrit gave forty acres to two thousand people.

Gerrit was a good steward of his mansion, too. He opened his home in Peterboro, New York to everyone who came to visit. He wrote in his journal one night

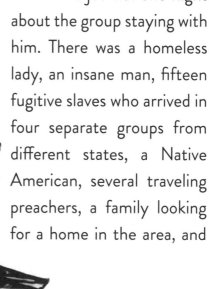

about the group staying with him. There was a homeless lady, an insane man, fifteen fugitive slaves who arrived in four separate groups from different states, a Native American, several traveling preachers, a family looking for a home in the area, and a man escorting six disabled children. Gerrit served Jesus by offering hospitality to all people at all times.

Lewis and Arthur Tappan, two brothers who loved Jesus, were friends with Gerrit Smith. The Tappans were businessmen who cared a lot about education and helped fund colleges to train preachers—like Oberlin College and Lane Theological Seminary. The schools taught that slavery is a sin, and many students became abolitionists. Calvin Fairbank graduated from Oberlin College. He went on to be a preacher and a

conductor on the Underground Railroad. Calvin spent nineteen years in prison as punishment for his good work, but he helped free nearly fifty slaves.

While Arthur concentrated on abolition, Lewis Tappan helped found the American Missionary Association to send missionaries to the refugees of slavery in Jamaica, Africa, and Canada, as well as to Native Americans in the United States. The association also set up schools for black students in the South during the Civil War, with over a thousand teachers coming from the North to help newly freed black children learn to read and write.

The Underground Railroad—and the passengers arriving in free areas—had a lot of needs. Because there were people who loved Jesus and who believed in stewarding his blessings well, there was always someone to provide a pair of shoes, a blank check, or even a parcel of land.

EXTRA POSTAGE

Henry Brown couldn't figure out how to get on the Underground Railroad. He was determined to leave slavery and loved Jesus deeply. Maybe he was praying when he decided to mail himself to William Still at the Philadelphia Anti-Slavery Office. Henry recruited a white merchant and a free black Underground Railroad conductor in Virginia to nail him into a wooden box just barely big enough to fit him.

Henry's trip from wagon to train to steamer and back to wagon and train was harrowing. Though the box was marked "This Side Up," Henry spent much of his trip upside down. He thought his eyes would explode. After twenty-seven hours, Henry arrived in

Philadelphia where several men pried the lid off the box. Henry stood, said "How do you do, gentlemen?" then fainted. When he awoke he sang, "I waited patiently for the Lord."

A PLACE
TO REST

As newly liberated people traveled to freedom, they needed safe houses where they could spend the day, like Gerrit Smith's mansion in New York. Because fugitives traveled at night—slave catchers were less likely to see them in the dark—stations on the Underground Railroad worked best if they were spaced about ten or twenty miles apart. In the early days of the Railroad, though, fugitives sometimes had to travel a hundred miles or more between stops. They risked getting lost or re-kidnapped on the way to freedom.

As the Railroad grew and developed, more stops were added. Communities formed by newly freed blacks also became stations to the Railroad. Now, not every station was as nice as Gerrit's mansion. Fugitives also stayed in barns, caves, attics, even piles of hay. Anywhere people could hide runaway slaves, they did.

Josiah Henson first heard the good news of Jesus at the age of eighteen. He was excited to hear that God loved all people, black and white. Josiah would one day become a pastor, leading people to Christ. He would serve as a conductor on the Railroad, leading one hundred eighteen people to freedom. He would also run one of the terminals in Canada. First, though, he had to free both himself, his wife, Charlotte, and their four children.

As Josiah and his family fled Kentucky, he carried two of his boys in a bag on his back. They were just too little to make the trip on foot. A fellow slave rowed the family across the Ohio River in the middle of the night. They were headed to Cincinnati, one hundred and fifty miles away.

Like many fugitives, the family didn't know about the Underground Railroad, so they hid in the forest during the day. After nearly two weeks on the road, they ran out of food. Josiah began knocking on doors for help, but found none. In Cincinnati, the Henson family finally found the Railroad and stayed at a station before taking a ride for thirty miles in a wagon toward Lake Erie. It must have been a relief to get off their feet after all that walking. Next, the Hensons stayed in a Native American wigwam.

They were conducted by warriors to a boat headed toward Buffalo, New York. Finally, they reached Canada. Josiah rolled on the ground, kissing handfuls of sand. The Henson family was free.

Fortunate travelers encountered stations early on their trip. Station masters let the next station know fugitives were on the way by sending messages in code. Christians at the next stop knew they should expect "friends," "packages," and "shipments." Some stations advertised they were open for business with subtle signals like a white cloth on a pole that meant all was safe. Reverend

John Rankin pulled a light up a flagpole in the yard of his house high on a hill over the Ohio River. That way, people escaping Kentucky knew it was safe to seek help there.

A light also shone in the attic of a big home overlooking the Niagara River, just seven miles north of Niagara Falls, in Lewiston, New York. Canada was just fifteen hundred feet across the river. Reverend Amos Tryon built the huge home with four cellars for his wife, Sally, and their ten kids. Sally didn't want to move into the home—she liked living in town. So, Amos' brother Josiah and his wife, Mary, bought the house.

The small two-hundred-person town of Lewiston was crawling with slave catchers in the 1830s. Josiah was a wonderful tailor who made beautiful, brightly colored jackets to present to the slave catchers as gifts. Not only did the men never suspect their friend, Josiah, of hiding fugitives, their beautiful jackets made them really easy to see coming. The townspeople, who decided to work on the Underground Railroad during a Christian revival, used to call Josiah the "man with the rainbow heart" because of his jackets.

Josiah hid up to thirty fugitives in his basement during the day. At night, Mary would give each fugitive a thick wool cape and a winter coat with some food in a bag. Then, Josiah led them sixty feet down the hillside into his rowboat. Over the years, Josiah rowed thousands to Canada where they became free.

Lines on the Underground Railroad were formed around stations throughout the North. Many churches housed fugitives, like the African Methodist Episcopal (AME) churches in major cities. The Mount Zion United AME Church in Washington DC used a burial vault in the church cemetery to hide freedom seekers during the day. Can you imagine hiding in a cemetery?

Pastors, too, opened their homes to passengers on the Railroad. In Tabor, Iowa, Reverend John Todd, a father of eight, built a hidden room the size of a closet where he hid people. In Ann Arbor, Michigan, Methodist minister Guy Beckley and his wife, Phyla, hid fugitives in their home with their eight children. Congregational minister George B. Hitchcock and his wife, Carolyn, welcomed freedom seekers into their Lewis, Iowa stone house built specifically to be a stop on the Underground Railroad, complete with a hidden basement room. Across the North, people who loved Jesus opened their homes to those fleeing slavery.

HIDING IN PLAIN SIGHT

Few enslaved people escaped the Deep South. Those who traveled thousands of miles out of the most southern states were often sailors, sailing out of the Gulf of Mexico. Ellen Craft, though, had an idea. She was light skinned enough to pose as a rich white man.

Ellen, though, didn't have a beard, a deep voice, nor could she sign her name. So, Ellen cut her hair and wrapped her head with a bandage. She put her arm in a sling, held a cane in the opposite hand, donned dark green glasses, and pretended to be deaf. Her husband, William, posed as a slave caring for his sickly master.

Ellen and William traveled a thousand miles by train, boat, and carriage, staying in first class hotels. Once they arrived in Philadelphia, the Underground Railroad forwarded them to Boston. Years later, William published their story.

THE LIGHT
IS ON

As station masters helped passengers,
they also recruited more abolitionists.
After all, the Underground Railroad

always needed people to purchase tickets, run stations, sew clothes, and pass information along. Conductors— people who escorted passengers to the next station, or who brought fugitives from the South into the North—also had to be recruited.

Reverend John Rankin recruited hundreds of people to abolition work in the town of Ripley, Ohio— including many of his own church members. When John preached God's Word each week, he frequently taught that work is one of God's good gifts. Everyone should do their own work or pay someone else a fair wage to do the work for them. John and his wife, Jean, believed in God's good gift of children as well. Every one of the thirteen Rankin children helped serve fugitive slaves in the big Rankin house on the hill overlooking the Ohio River. The family helped around three thousand people.

Each night, Jean and her four daughters prepared food, stoked the fire, and made beds. The barn often had ten or more people hiding, ready to travel with one or two of the nine Rankin boys who worked as conductors during the middle of the night. The boys took fugitives twenty-one miles north through the forest to a station in Sardinia, Ohio. Can you imagine traveling all night, then walking one hundred steps down the hill to school, acting cheerful so no one will know you're tired? That's just what those boys did each night.

Being a station master was a dangerous job. Reverend John was worth twenty-five hundred dollars—dead. One night, Calvin Rankin and his cousin saw suspicious men in town. At two in the morning, they heard a whistle outside, so the boys snuck out the back door with pistols. Both came face to face with sneaky intruders, who fired pistols at them, but missed. Well, that night was a mess. There were more

shots fired, the barn was set on fire, and everyone in town rushed up the hill to save the Rankin family from Kentucky slave catchers.

A five-day walk to the west, in Madison, Indiana, nearly all members of the Underground Railroad were Baptist, free, and black. The middle-class business owners were blacksmiths, they ran farmer's markets and laundries, or—like George DeBaptiste—they cut hair. When enslaved people came into Madison to have pigs turned into sausage, businessmen whispered in their ears about freedom. Anyone who

wanted to be free was ushered out of town by these same prosperous black men armed with pistols. Then, George would return to his barbershop to cut the hair of slave owners, until his next unsuspecting passenger came in for a quick haircut.

Jermain Loguen's master attacked him with a block of wood, badly scarring his mouth and altering the way he talked. After a harrowing journey from Tennessee to Canada, Jermain learned to read and write, then moved to Syracuse, New York where he became a pastor with the African Methodist Episcopal Zion denomination. Jermain and his wife Caroline had six children together.

Jermain and Caroline brought two hundred people each year through their home. They were constantly exhausted, opening the door to fugitives each night, even when their thirteen-year-old daughter, Latitia, was dying from tuberculosis. Once, Jermain opened the door to find Frederick Douglass standing on the front stoop with nine fugitives. Frederick found the group at the Central Railroad Station in Syracuse that ran through the center of the city.

Now, in Syracuse, New York, the Underground Railroad was anything but "underground." The city leaders decided that if slave catchers ever used the

Central Railroad to re-enslave people by sending them south on the train, the whole council would pull the rails off the street with their own hands. Jermain was above-ground, too. He even took out ads in local newspapers telling people to come to him for help.

Like George DeBaptiste, William Still was born free. The youngest of eighteen children, William's mother was a fugitive. Three years after William moved from New Jersey to the massive city of Philadelphia, he married a lady named Letitia and they shared four children. William was so good at his job as the clerk for the local abolition society that when the 1850 Fugitive Slave Law passed, he became chairman of the vigilance committee in Philadelphia.

William, a Presbyterian church elder, helped enslaved people escape from faraway places, like Virginia and the nation's capital in Washington, DC. He kept detailed records of every runaway who came through his station, including his meeting with a man named Peter Friedman. Peter, who was twenty years older than William, escaped from Alabama. He looked familiar in a strange we've-never-met kind of way. As William interviewed Peter, he realized this wasn't just another fugitive—Peter was William's own brother. God blessed both men that day.

Being a station master on the Underground Railroad was hard, dangerous work. Station masters often found their homes raided or even attacked by slave catchers. Being exposed as a station master could mean jail, fines, or death. Station masters, though, could save hundreds or even thousands from bondage—sometimes even their own family members.

CHANGING MINDS

"How terrible!" exclaimed Harriet Beecher Stowe as she sat next to her husband, a Bible professor. Across from them, Reverend John Rankin was explaining how a fugitive woman had jumped across the Ohio River on pieces of thick ice while clinging to her baby. Fourteen years after her late-night flight, Stowe retold the woman's story through the character Eliza in her bestselling novel, *Uncle Tom's Cabin.*

Stowe's novel sold three hundred thousand copies during its first year in the United States—and a million copies in England. Based on real stories, the novel's depiction of the hardship slaves endured created a public debate. Frederick Douglass felt the novel helped people understand how horrible slavery really was. Harriet Tubman refused to even see one of the many plays based on the novel, saying she'd seen the real suffering of her people—she didn't need to see it acted out.

ALL ABOARD!

Conductors often had the most difficult—and most dangerous—job on the Underground Railroad. Without satellite maps, or any maps at all, with no road signs, and often without even a safe dirt road to travel, conductors took Railroad passengers from one station to the next.

Some conductors even went deep into the South to run off slaves—they brought enslaved people from the southern states into the North.

Conductors worked with station masters across the North. They also secretly collaborated with enslaved people who were willing to help free fellow slaves. A slave catcher from Kentucky by the name of Peter Driscoll looked for fugitives in the border states so he could re-enslave them. Ironically, Peter had no idea that his own slaves were helping people escape as Peter was busy searching for fugitives. Later, Peter's slaves also escaped to Canada.

Most conductors couldn't work in that position for more than ten years. The stress and anxiety from the constant danger  proved to be too much for even the bravest underground workers. Calvin Fairbank loved Jesus and hated slavery from an early age. While working on the Ohio River one day, twenty-two-year-old Calvin gave an enslaved man a quick ride across the river to freedom. That started a long career of guiding men and women to freedom, usually in disguises. Five years after becoming a conductor, Calvin was ordained as a minister.

The first time Pastor Calvin was caught, he was loading a Kentucky waiter into a horse-drawn carriage along with his wife and child. The family escaped, but Calvin returned to Kentucky—to free more people— and was arrested. Calvin spent five years preaching the gospel to other prisoners. Even after prison, Calvin just wouldn't stop helping people escape bondage. None of his forty-seven passengers were ever caught, but Calvin wasn't so fortunate. He spent a total of seventeen years in prison. Calvin was flogged—beaten with a whip—over thirty-five thousand times while in prison.

Harriet Tubman escaped slavery to become the most famous Underground Railroad conductor. One day, Harriet's niece Kessiah and her two children stood on the courthouse steps during a Maryland auction. They were purchased by a black man in the crowd. This probably wasn't unusual. Free black men sometimes owned slaves, while some trusted household slaves might acquire new slaves on behalf of their white owners. The auctioneers waited for payment before realizing Kessiah and her children were missing. Meanwhile, Kessiah's husband, John Bowley—the auction winner, was hurrying his family to Baltimore where Harriet put them on the train north to freedom. Harriet made thirteen trips south to rescue around seventy people, including most of her family.

Harriet loved God and trusted her safety to him. Self-educated Underground Railroad men, like station master William Still and abolitionist Frederick Douglass, considered her simple country ways to be a little embarrassing, but they admired her courage and wisdom. Harriet couldn't read or write, but she was a master of disguise. She would carry props with

her, like a bunch of chickens. If Harriet thought she was about to be discovered, she would stoop over her basket like an old woman or aggravate her chickens until they flapped their wings in front of her face. No one paid any attention to the tiny "old" lady with the crazy chickens.

Conductor John P. Parker was also a former slave. John and his wife, Miranda, settled in busy Ripley, Ohio where Reverend Rankin's family ran their hilltop station. The Christian couple had six kids together. Each night, John walked along the riverfront, looking for people on the other side who needed a ride. John found more than seven hundred people to help. John also went into Kentucky to run off fugitives. With a bounty of one thousand dollars on his head, his dangerous work nearly cost him his life more than once.

One night, John heard through the Railroad grapevine that ten Kentucky fugitives needed help. A friend dropped John on the Kentucky river shore, armed with two pistols and a knife. Once John found the group, he and his passengers were pursued by a gang of slave catchers who patrolled the river.

Now, the Ohio River at Ripley was full of flatboats, rowboats, and steamboats during the day. That night, John took a rowboat from the shore. Everyone tried to pile into the boat, but there wasn't room, so several men stayed on shore. In Ripley, the one hundred steps up the hill to the Rankin farm were too dangerous to climb out in the open with slave catchers chasing them, so John took his passengers to the pastor of a

church five miles outside of town. From there, they were sent to the next station on the Railroad.

Conductors on the Underground Railroad had a difficult job, and the price of failure was high. Although many successful conductors became station masters in the North when they no longer wanted to travel into the South, Harriet Tubman took an even more dangerous job as a spy for the Union Army during the Civil War.

Christian workers on the railroad disagreed over the morality of conducting enslaved people out of the South. After all, the job often involved deception and, sometimes, theft.

Conductors, though, believed that enslaved people had been gravely sinned against. They felt they were following the law of God over the laws of men.

ENSLAVED TO FREE OTHERS

Because he was enslaved, nineteen-year-old Arnold Gragston could legally be beaten—or even murdered. He worried about what could happen to him if he rowed the pretty girl in front of him across the Ohio River to Ripley. But, he couldn't let her get in trouble, so as he rowed he concentrated on the light at the top of the pole up on the Rankin farm.

Arnold remained enslaved four years while he took three or four hundred fugitives across the water on

moonless nights. During his last trip, Arnold saw slave catchers waiting for him to return to Kentucky. So, Arnold lived in the woods, sleeping in trees until he and his wife could escape. After the Civil War, the Gragston family lived in Detroit where Arnold told his ten kids and thirty-one grandchildren stories of his adventures as a conductor on the Underground Railroad.

LAST STOP!

Every good train ride must eventually come to an end. Most passengers on the Underground Railroad didn't know where they were going when they started their journey. They were just looking for a life that was better than one lived in bondage.

Newly freed people began to form communities. While some enslaved people found freedom in Mexico, Haiti, or even in maroon colonies like the Dismal Swamp, most fled north. There, they found refuge in little rural communities, in neighborhoods of the big cities, or in Canada.

In rural areas, African American farming communities formed. Fugitives in New Jersey from a place called Snow Hill, Maryland named their new home after the place where they had once been enslaved. Peter Mott was the pastor at Snow Hill. Right away, Peter built a big, two-story house. You could have fit four regular slave cabins inside Peter and his wife, Elizabeth Ann's, house. The Mott family fit Railroad passengers inside, instead—lots and lots of passengers.

Close to Snow Hill, about one hundred and twenty-five African Americans owned farms in an area called Timbuctoo. When a slave catcher showed up with his minions to kidnap Timbuctoo resident Perry Simmons just before the Civil War, Perry defended himself with two rifles and an axe. Word of his predicament quickly spread, and the town rushed to Perry's defense in what would later be called the Battle of Pine Swamp.

There were other black islands—African American farming communities—like Pokepatch in Ohio, Lick Creek Settlement in Indiana, and New Philadelphia in Illinois. They served as stations on the Underground Railroad for people headed further north, and as terminals for those who wanted to live quiet, ordinary lives in the country of their birth.

Some passengers settled in black neighborhoods in large cities, like Boston in Massachusetts, Cincinnati in Ohio, Philadelphia in Pennsylvania, and New York City. Life in the crowded cities could be difficult for African Americans. Because slavery had become racially based at that time and place in history, blacks living in America faced a lot of racism, even in the cities.

African American children often couldn't attend public schools, though their parents paid taxes for them. Black adults were often not allowed to vote, and the government did not consider them to be citizens, even though they were born in the United States where they lived and worked their entire lives. Some jobs refused to hire black people. Many services, like boats, trains, and even churches, were segregated—blacks and whites had separate seating.

Now, the Bible tells us that all people are made in the image of God. Jesus tells us to love God and to love our neighbors as ourselves. God tells us he formed each of us in the womb. To divide God's people from each other or to deny people schooling, church, or transportation based on the color of their skin is a sin.

Blacks and whites worked together to fix the racism— hatred and discrimination based on skin color—that African Americans lived with. Teachers opened schools for black children. Pastors and abolitionists talked about what God says in the Bible about loving your neighbor and about how God hates the slave trade.

Sojourner Truth, an abolitionist who had once been enslaved, insisted on riding the streetcar, even though she was black. The driver refused, but Sojourner insisted until she was finally allowed on public transportation. The Civil War ended slavery in America, but people— both blacks and whites—would continue to work against racism for more than one hundred years after the fighting ended. That fight started in the northern cities.

In Canada, American fugitives were legally free. They set up communities they could expect to last.

Josiah Henson, who fled slavery with his two youngest children in a bag on his back, worked as a conductor out of Canada, leading one hundred and eighteen slaves to freedom. Using money he earned, Josiah purchased two hundred acres for his family.

Over time, Josiah learned to read and write, becoming a Methodist minister. As more people arrived in Canada, Josiah became convinced that education and the ability to work were the keys to becoming truly free. Josiah developed a plan with Hiram Wilson, a white missionary from New Hampshire. They would create a boarding school in their Dawn Settlement that would teach boys academic subjects and the skills to earn a living. Girls would learn to care for a household and garden.

Josiah and Hiram used money raised by James Canning Fuller to purchase two hundred acres along the Syndenham River in Ontario. In November 1841, Josiah, Hiram, and settlers in Dawn kneeled

in deep snow and gave thanks to God for his provision. Then, they got to work. A year later, the British-American Institute opened with twelve students. Hiram taught academics while Josiah taught Bible to the students. By the late 1840s, sixty to eighty students at a time lived and studied at the school. Dawn had five hundred settlers on fifteen hundred acres of farmland. They worked making rope, grinding grain, making bricks, and sawing lumber.

Throughout America and Canada, refugees from slavery worked to create communities where they could live, learn, worship, and thrive.

THE ABOVE GROUND RAILROAD

After the passage of the 1850 Fugitive Slave Law, perhaps twenty thousand northern African Americans fled into Canada. One New York church only had two members remaining. When people were captured in northern states, angry crowds stormed prisons and courthouses. In 1851, a large group freed Daniel in

Buffalo, Jerry Henry in Syracuse—both in New York, and Shadrach Minkins from Boston, Massachusetts. All three men fled to Canada.

In 1860, Charles Nalle was arrested by a slave catcher in Troy, New York. Harriet Tubman pushed her way into the bank where Charles was being held and a huge crowd gathered. Harriet clung to Charles while officials beat her over the head. Abolitionists rowed Charles across the Hudson River while the crowd followed in a ferry and rowboats. Both groups fired guns at each other. Charles escaped just before the United States went to war, North against South.

UNDERGROUND RAILROAD: THE TRUTH

How do we know what happened in history? Much of history occurred a long time ago, and often there are no living eyewitnesses—people who have personally seen an event—to tell us what happened. When we can interview two or three eyewitnesses, we can be reasonably certain we understand what happened.

For history from a long time ago, historians use historical objects and documents to understand what occurred. Each document is like a puzzle piece. It only shows a little bit of the historical picture. Every document has some bias—the ideas and worldview of each author influences what information they include and how they write about it. Historians must piece history together using the best documents available.

Enslaved people who escaped sometimes wrote slave narratives. Those stories are specifically from the point of view of the author and only cover their own life experience. Narratives help us understand what riding the Underground Railroad was like for an individual person.

Slave owners also created puzzle pieces for the history of the Underground Railroad with advertisements they would publish in newspapers every time they wanted to find an enslaved person who had disappeared. These ads detail fugitive names, ages, and physical descriptions. We learn about personality, too, from the ads.

Most conductors and station masters did not keep written records of their work because they could be used in a court of law. William Still, though, conducted detailed interviews with fugitives helped by the Vigilant Committee of Philadelphia. He recorded where each person came from, their names and family history, how they escaped, and who helped them. William hid his records in a vault in an old cemetery. After the Civil War, he published the stories of six hundred and forty-nine newly free fugitives. Their stories help us understand much about the Underground Railroad and how it worked. William's work shows that African Americans were heavily involved in the Underground Railroad.

Nearly forty years after slavery was abolished in the United States, a young history professor, Wilbur H. Siebert, spent forty years researching and writing about the Underground Railroad. Professor Wilbur sent hundreds of letters all over the North, asking people what they remembered about their family's involvement with the Underground Railroad. He was looking for stories, routes of escape, and names of station masters and conductors.

Hundreds of people replied. Their written memories, maps, and information filled thirty-eight volumes. Wilbur compiled his research into a book, published in 1898. He also developed a map he called the "Underground Routes to Canada" with many stations on the map.

Wilbur's *The Underground Railroad* research shows how historians can display bias. You see, he most often asked white people for memories of their parents and grandparents. Though the professor's final research contained more stories of blacks working on the Railroad than of whites, most of the important work done by African Americans was left out. Fugitives were treated as a group, rather than as individuals with names and histories. Wilbur also didn't research any of the stories to make sure they were true.

The United States Government also got involved in recording stories of the Underground Railroad from 1936 to 1937, more than seventy years after the end of the Civil War. The government paid journalists to

interview former slaves and record their answers. These interviews are another way that historians can learn about abolition, slavery, and the Railroad. The people interviewed must have been fairly young while enslaved, since every American was freed from slavery just after the war.

Even with the late start to the project, journalists located more than two thousand people who had actually been enslaved and interviewed them for the project. They also took five hundred photographs. In 1941, seventeen volumes of short slave narratives were published. That's how you were able to learn about the story of Arnold Gragston who remained enslaved for four years in order to free hundreds of people from Kentucky and Tennessee. Arnold was interviewed by a journalist named Pearl Randolph and photographed. He was nearly one hundred years old by the time he spoke to Pearl.

History detectives, like you, can piece together the puzzle of history through artifacts, personal narratives, research from historians like Professor Wilbur H. Siebert, and interviews with eyewitnesses like those recorded by William Still and Pearl Randolph. As you read and learn, you will be able to make connections between people, events, and movements. History is a little like a spiderweb. Everything touches something else in some way.

The most important thing we see as we learn about history is how our extraordinary God worked through his ordinary people. God uses people just like you to accomplish his purposes all the time. They are people who love their neighbors just as much as they love themselves.

People who obey God, not man, change the course of history. They don't change it all at once. No, history is changed just a little at a time, one heart at a time. The most important thing people who love Jesus can do is tell others about the love of Jesus. We can tell them that Jesus died and rose again to pay the punishment for the sins of all who repent and believe in him.

GOD'S WORD:
THE TRUTH

Our understanding of history may change as we uncover new documents or remember important truths—like the truth that kidnapping and selling human souls is outlawed in God's Word (Exodus 21:16). Human laws change as culture and rulers change. God's Word never changes.

We know God's Word is true because God tells us it is. New evidence—like additional manuscripts—always prove God's Word can be trusted. Think about what 2 Timothy 3:16-17, says: "All Scripture is breathed out by God and profitable for teaching, for reproof, for correction, and for training in righteousness, that the man of God may be complete, equipped for every good work."

We obey God, not man. Disobeying man's law is serious and should be done only after searching the Bible and praying. We can trust that the Holy Spirit will guide us as we work to understand God's Word.

TIMELINE

1775

The American Revolution begins. American and British armies promise freedom if enslaved African Americans fight. British kept their promise and freed soldiers.

1776

The Declaration of Independence is signed on July 4th.

1780

Northern states begin freeing enslaved Americans.

1783

Americans win the Revolutionary War against the British and become an independent nation, the United States of America.

1783

George Liele arrives in Jamaica with the British.

1787

The first two steamboats are sailed in America.

1804

The Louisiana Purchase adds a great deal of land to the United States—and more slave territory.

1807

The U.K. Slave Trade Abolition Act bans the importation of slaves onto American soil. The domestic slave trade—buying and selling humans within the U.S.—continues.

1819

Britain declares all enslaved people entering Canada are free and not eligible for recapture.

1820s

African Americans begin setting up vigilance committees to help freedom seekers.

1822

Reverend John Rankin moves to Ripley, Ohio to become a station master there.

1830

The first train track is laid in Baltimore. Josiah and Charlotte Henson reach Canada with their four children.

1831

Train travel takes off in America with the 100-mile Mohawk & Hudson Railroad and an improved steam locomotive. Tice Davids escapes by swimming across the Ohio River and disappearing on the "underground road."

1833

Arthur Tappan and William Lloyd Garrison found the American Anti-Slavery Society.

1834

Jermain Loguen escapes from Tennessee to Canada on a stolen horse after being assaulted by his owner.

1835

America experiences forty-six pro-slavery riots.

Josiah and Mary Tryon use the house on the Niagara River to shelter freedom seekers as Josiah rows thousands to freedom in Canada.

1836

Jermain Loguen moves to New York and runs the Underground Railroad in Syracuse.

1838

Frederick Douglass escapes from Baltimore dressed as a sailor.

George DeBaptiste moves to Madison, Indiana and serves as a station master.

Calvin Fairbank rescues an enslaved man for the first time. He later spends seventeen years in prison for conducting people to freedom.

Josiah Henson and Hiram Wilson establish the British-American Institute.

1840

The US House of Representatives enacts the Gag Rule, prohibiting the reception or consideration of antislavery petitions.

1841

Reverend John Rankin's home and family are attacked in Ripley, Ohio.

1842

Reverend Guy Beckley and his wife, Phyla, build a home in Ann Arbor, Michigan and hide freedom seekers.

1845

Pastor Peter Mott builds his home which serves as a station at Snow Hill, New Jersey.

1846

Gerrit Smith gifts forty acres to each of two thousand African Americans.

Lewis Tappan helps found the American Missionary Association.

1847

William Still begins working for the Pennsylvania Society for the Abolition of Slavery. He becomes the chairman of the vigilance committee there after the passage of the 1850 Fugitive Slave Law.

1848

Ellen and William Craft escape North from Georgia wearing disguises.

1849

Harriet Tubman escapes from Maryland to Philadelphia.

Henry "Box" Brown mails himself to Philadelphia from Virginia.

Ellen and William Craft escape from Georgia to Boston.

1850

September 18 – The Fugitive Slave Act endangers all black people in the United States, both enslaved and free. It also forces whites to act as slave catchers.

Harriet Tubman helps free her niece, Kessiah, and Kessiah's two children.

John P. Parker moves to Ripley, Ohio and begins his work as a conductor.

1851

Abolitionists free Jerry Henry from slave catchers by storming a prison in Syracuse.

In Boston, Shadrach Minkins is freed by a mob invading a prison.

1852

Harriet Beecher Stowe's novel, Uncle Tom's Cabin, becomes an immediate bestseller.

1853

Reverend John and Martha Todd build their home in Tabor, Iowa, where they shelter fugitives.

1854

The Kansas-Nebraska Act allows additional western territory added to the United States to self-determine its slavery status.

Pastor George B. Hitchcock builds a home in Lewis, Iowa with a secret room in the basement.

Abolitionists overwhelm slave catchers in Milwaukee, Wisconsin, freeing Joshua Glover.

1857

The Dred Scott Decision at the Supreme Court protects southern slavery and declares blacks can not become citizens.

1859

Arnold Gragston begins working as a conductor on the Underground Railroad. He remains enslaved for four years to help others.

1861

John Brown tries to overthrow the United States Government by attacking Harper's Ferry in West Virginia. He is executed.

1861-1865

The American Civil War brings an end to slavery in the United States.

1863

Arnold Gragston makes his last trip as a conductor across the Ohio River.

1865

April – President Abraham Lincoln assassinated. The Thirteenth Amendment abolishes slavery in the United States.

1868

The Fourteenth Amendment prohibits racial discrimination in laws.

1870

The Fifteenth Amendment prohibits denying the right to vote based on color, race, or previous condition of slavery.

1872

William Still publishes the stories of 649 fugitives in his book, The Underground Railroad.

1898

Wilbur H. Siebert publishes his research in a book also titled The Underground Railroad.

1936-1937

The United States of America sends reporters to interview former slaves about slavery.

WORKS CONSULTED

Andres, Jane. "Seldom-heard story of Tryon's Folly." The Niagara-on-the-Lake Local. February 24, 2021. https://notllocal.com/2021/02/24/seldom-heard-story-of-tryons-folly/. Accessed 6/29/2022.

Anonymous, ed. *The Great Abolitionists: Sojourner Truth, John Brown, William Lloyd Garrison, Harriet Beecher Stowe, Frederick Douglass, Harriet Tubman*. A.J. Cornell Publications, 2019.

"Baltimore & Ohio Railroad." Case Western Reserve University. https://case.edu/ech/articles/b/baltimore-ohio-railroad. Accessed 6/28/2022.

Blaisdell, Bob and Christine Rudisel, editors. *Slave Narratives of the Underground Railroad*. Dover Publications, Inc., 2014.

Blight, David, ed. *Passages to Freedom: The Underground Railroad in History and Memory*. Harper Paperbacks, 2006.

Bordewich, Fergus M. *Bound for Canaan: The Epic Story of the Underground Railroad, America's First Civil Rights Movement*. Amistad, 2006.

Bradford, Sarah. Harriet Tubman: *The Moses of Her People*. Dover Publications, 2004. (Original work published 1869.)

Calarco, Tom. *People of the Underground Railroad: A Biographical Dictionary*. Greenwood Press, 2008.

Deibert, Brannon. "Who Are the Quakers? 7 Facts About Their History & Beliefs." Christianity.com. https://www.christianity.com/church/denominations/the-quakers-7-things-about-their-history-beliefs.html. Accessed 5/24/2022.

Drescher, Seymour. *Abolition: A History of Slavery and Antislavery*. Cambridge University Press, 2009.

Duncan, Dr. Ligon. "Defending the Faith; Denying the Image: 19th Century American Confessional Calvinism in Faithfulness and Failure" Gospel Reformation Network. May 16, 2018. https://

gospelreformation.net/defending-the-faith-denying-the-image/. Accessed 9/20/2020.

Duncan, Dr. Ligon. "What About Slavery?" Reformed Theological Seminary. https://rts.edu/resources/what-about-slavery/. Accessed 9/20/2020.

Franklin, John Hope and Moss, Alfred A., Jr. *From Slavery to Freedom: A History of African Americans.* McGraw-Hill Higher Education, 2000.

"Freedom Crossing." Historic Lewiston, New York. https://historiclewiston.org/freedomcrossing/. Accessed 6/28/2022.

Gayle, Clement. *George Liele: Pioneer Missionary to Jamaica.* Bethlehem Book Publishers, Inc., 2002.

Greene, Nelson, ed. "Chapter 87: History of the New York Central Railroad and Other Valley Lines." History of the Mohawk Valley: Gateway to the West 1614-1925, Volume II. The S. J. Clarke Publishing Company, 1925, pp. 1288-1306. Schenectady Digital History Archive, http://www.schenectadyhistory.org/resources/mvgw/history/087.html.

Grun, Bernard. *The Timetables of History.* Simon & Schuster, 1963.

"Guy Beckley House, 1842." Ann Arbor District Library. https://aadl.org/buildings_1425pontiac. Accessed 6/29/2022.

"History." The Reverend George B. Hitchcock House. http://hitchcockhouse.org/wordpress2018/history/. Accessed 6/29/2022.

Hudson, J. Blaine. *Encyclopedia of the Underground Railroad.* McFarland & Company, 2006.

"John P. Parker, Conductor, on the Underground Railroad." History Matters. http://historymatters.gmu.edu/d/6232/. Accessed 7/6/2022.

Menikoff, Aaron. "How and Why Did Some Christians Defend Slavery?" The Gospel Coalition. February 24, 2017. https://www.thegospelcoalition.org/article/how-and-why-did-some-christians-defend-slavery/. Accessed 9/20/2020.

Newman, Richard S. *Abolitionism: A Very Short Introduction*. Oxford University Press, 2018.

Ross, Mark. "Imago Dei." Ligonier. March 25, 2013. https://www. ligonier.org/learn/articles/imago-dei. Accessed 6/5/2022.

Shannon, Sr., David T., Sr. Ed., Deborah Van Broekhoven & Julia Frazier White, Ed. *George Liele's Life and Legacy: An Unsung Hero*. Mercer University Press, 2012.

Sharp, Joshua. "Voices: There is no biblical defense for American slavery." Baptist Standard. January 27, 2020. https://www. baptiststandard.com/opinion/voices/no-biblical-defense-american-slavery/. Accessed 9/20/2020.

Sinha, Manisha. *The Slave's Cause: A History of Abolition*. Yale University Press, 2016.

Still, William, and Quincy T. Mills, editor. *The Underground Railroad Records: Narrating the Hardships, Hairbreadth Escapes, and Death Struggles of Slaves in Their Efforts for Freedom*. Modern Library, 2019.

"The Beginnings of American Railroads and Mapping." Library of Congress. https://www.loc.gov/collections/railroad-maps-1828-to-1900/articles-and-essays/history-of-railroads-and-maps/the-beginnings-of-american-railroads-and-mapping/. Accessed 6/28/2022.

"The Todd House." Tabor Historical Society. https://www. taboriowahistoricalsociety.org/todd-house-museum. Accessed 6/29/2022.

"Tom Thumb." B&O Railroad Museum. https://www.borail.org/collection/tom-thumb/. Accessed 6/28/2022.

"When is civil disobedience allowed for a Christian?" Got Questions. https://www.gotquestions.org/civil-disobedience.html. Accessed 6/28/2022.

Danika has done it again! Built on the foundation of God's command to love our neighbors as ourselves, in her Who, What, Why series, Danika comprehensively explores the tragic history of slavery throughout time and throughout the world. It's a sad history, but also a hopeful one, with God's gracious promise ultimately to set captives free.

Douglas Bond
Author of more than thirty books,
including *War in the Wasteland*, and *The Resistance*

In this book, Danika Cooley gives us a fascinating account of the early years of trains and railroads in America. It was the ugly days of slavery and slave trading. So, the language used in the locomotive industry was also employed in the freeing of slaves and conveying them to freedom. It was through the "underground railroad"! Young people need to read this captivating history that Cooley weaves together. It will enable them to see what it means to practically love their neighbours in a cruel world.

Conrad Mbewe
Pastor of Kabwata Baptist Church and founding chancellor
of the African Christian University in Lusaka, Zambia

Danika Cooley had hit the mark with this series. Slavery is an ugly topic, but the stories of the Christian responses to the evil allow hope to shine through. Readers will learn a lot of history, but more importantly they will learn what it means to put the Gospel into action. A series well worth reading.

Linda Finlayson
Author of *God's Timeline* and *God's Bible Timeline*

Why did the Reformation Happen?
Danika Cooley

The Church was following the words of men rather than the Word of God but brave men read God's Word and were saved from their sins. They fought for truth against the most powerful organizations of the time – the Church and the Crown. Danika Cooley explores how God's people changed the Church, Europe and the World. This is the story of how the Church found the gospel and the people heard about Christ.

ISBN: 978-1-5271-0652-9

Who What Why

Who was
Martin Luther?

Danika Cooley

Who was Martin Luther?
Danika Cooley

Martin Luther was a young man who was afraid of a thunderstorm. He was a monk seeking for salvation. He was a reformer who inspired a continent to return to the Word of God. Danika Cooley introduces 9–11 year olds to this key figure in the Reformation.

ISBN: 978-1-5271-0650-5

Who What Why

What was the Gutenberg Bible?

Danika Cooley

What was the Gutenberg Bible?

Danika Cooley

Johann Gutenberg invented a world–changing machine that meant people could read God's Word for themselves. The world could share ideas, discoveries and new and God's Word could be quickly, inexpensively and accurately reproduced. Danika Cooley helps 9–11 year–olds discover how the printing press paved the way for the Reformation.

ISBN: 978-1-5271-0651-2

Christian Focus Publications publishes books for adults and children under its four main imprints: Christian Focus, CF4K, Mentor and Christian Heritage. Our books reflect our conviction that God's Word is reliable and Jesus is the way to know him, and live for ever with him.

Our children's publication list covers pre-school to early teens. We also publish personal and family devotional titles, biographies and inspirational stories that children will love.

From pre-school board books to teenage apologetics, we have it covered!

Christian Focus Publications Ltd,
Geanies House, Fearn, Ross-shire,
IV20 1TW, Scotland,
United Kingdom.
www.christianfocus.com